FAMOUS LATINOS

César Chávez

Fighting for Fairness

Lila and Rick Guzmán

Enslow Elementary

an imprint of

Enslow Publishers, Inc.

40 Industrial Road
Box 398
Berkeley Heights, NJ 07922
USA

http://www.enslow.com

Series Adviser
Bárbara C. Cruz, Ed.D.
Professor, Social Science Education
University of South Florida

Series Literacy Consultant
Allan A. De Fina, Ph.D.
Past President of the New Jersey Reading Association
Professor, Department of Literacy Education
New Jersey City University

Note to Parents and Teachers: The *Famous Latinos* series supports National Council for the Social Studies (NCSS) curriculum standards. The Words to Know section introduces subject-specific vocabulary words.

This series was designed by Irasema Rivera, an award-winning Latina graphic designer.

Enslow Elementary, an imprint of Enslow Publishers, Inc.
Enslow Elementary® is a registered trademark of Enslow Publishers, Inc.

Library of Congress Cataloging-in-Publication Data

Lila, Guzmán, 1952–

    César Chávez : fighting for fairness / Lila and Rick Guzmán. — 1st ed.
      p. cm. — (Famous latinos)
    Includes index.
    ISBN 0-7660-2370-2 (hardcover)
    1. Chávez, César, 1927–1993. 1. Juvenile literature. 2. Labor leaders—United States—Biography—Juvenile literature. 3. Migrant agricultural laborers—Labor unions—United States—Officials and employees—Biography—Juvenile literature. 4. Mexican American migrant agricultural laborers—Biography—Juvenile literature. 5. United Farm Workers—History—Juvenile literature. I. Guzmán, Rick. II. Title. III. Series.
    HD6509.C48 L55 2006
    331.88'13'092—dc22
    [B]   2005031807

Printed in the United States of America

10 9 8 7 6 5 4 3 2 1

To Our Readers: We have done our best to make sure all Internet addresses in this book were active and appropriate when we went to press. However, the author and the publisher have no control over and assume no liability for the material available on those Internet sites or on other Web sites they may link to. Any comments or suggestions can be sent by e-mail to comments@enslow.com or to the address on the back cover.

Every effort has been made to locate all copyright holders of material used in this book. If any errors or omissions have occurred, corrections will be made in future editions of this book.

Illustration Credits: AP/Wide World, pp. 1, 4 (top), 10, 11, 22 (top right), 24 (both), 25 (both), 26, 27, 28; César E. Chávez Foundation, pp. 4 (bottom left, bottom right), 6, 12 (bottom), 13, 14, 15, 16; © Corel Corporation, 12 (top right); Enslow Publishers, pp. 8, 12 (top left); Hemera Technologies, 7, 22 (top left); Walter P. Reuther Library, Wayne State University, pp. 17, 19, 20, 21 (both), 22 (bottom).

Cover Photograph: AP/Wide World

❊ Contents ❊

César Chávez

Baby César

César and his older sister, Rita.

�֎ 1 ֎

On the Move

... hávez was a boy, he never lived in
... r very long. By the time he was
... e to more than thirty-six schools.
... ved from farm to farm, picking
... bles. They were called migrant
... ts. *Migrant* means "moving."
... family picked grapes and peas for
... the fields, the sun was burning hot.
... g. César did not think it was fair to
... earn so little. Would his life ever get
... always been like this.

Cesario Estrada Chávez, called César, was born
on March 31, 1927, at his grandparents' farm near

César and Rita dressed up in their best clothes for their first Holy Communion.

the town of Yuma, Arizona. César's father, Librado, ran a grocery store and a garage. César's mother, Juana, took care of the six children. The family lived in rooms above the store.

César had fun playing with his brothers and his sisters. But he was shy and did not like going to school. At home, his family spoke Spanish. At school, the teacher said César must learn English. She hit his knuckles with a ruler if he spoke Spanish.

In 1929, hard times hit the United States. All over the country, many stores, factories, and even banks went out of business. Librado had to close the store and move his family back to the farm.

On the farm, César chopped wood and fed the horses and chickens. He planted, watered, and weeded the fields of cotton, corn, and squash. On warm summer nights, the family sat together under the stars for supper. While they ate, César's grandmother told stories about his grandfather, a brave man who had been born in Mexico. His mother told stories from the Bible that taught him about right and wrong. From his mother and grandmother, César learned to stand up for what was right.

Soon, big troubles hit the Chávez farm. For a long time, there was no rain. Without water, the crops in the fields died. Then, in 1938, César's family did not have enough money to pay their bills. They had to leave the farm in Arizona. They packed up their car and went to California to find work. César was ten years old when he and his family became migrant farmworkers.

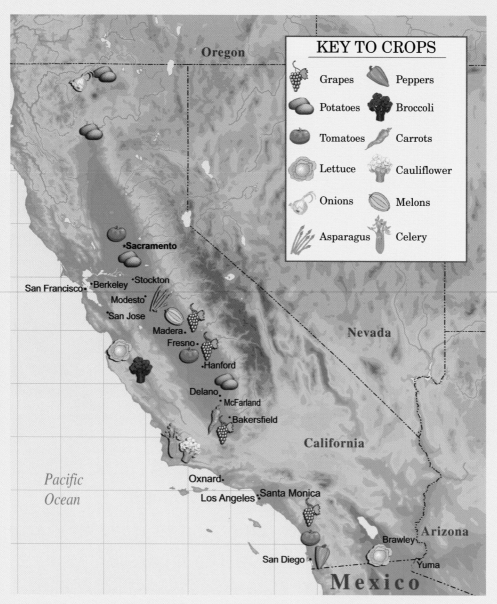

KEY TO CROPS

- Grapes
- Potatoes
- Tomatoes
- Lettuce
- Onions
- Asparagus
- Peppers
- Broccoli
- Carrots
- Cauliflower
- Melons
- Celery

Oregon

Sacramento
Berkeley · Stockton
San Francisco · Modesto
San Jose
Madera
Fresno
Hanford
Delano
McFarland
Bakersfield

Nevada

California

Pacific Ocean

Oxnard
Los Angeles · Santa Monica

Arizona
Brawley
San Diego
Yuma

Mexico

Migrants picked fruits and vegetables all over California.

❋2❋

Life in California

César and his family traveled all over California following the crops. When grapes were in season, they picked grapes. When tomatoes were ripe, they picked tomatoes. César and his family worked for many years picking all kinds of crops: tomatoes, plums, melons, berries, grapes, cotton, sugar beets, and lettuce.

The work was hard, especially when César had to dig out weeds with the short-handled hoe. He had to bend very low to use it. Migrant workers hated this tool. Bending over all the time hurt their backs.

Life was terrible for the migrants. César and his family often had to stay in cardboard shacks or tents.

They had no bathrooms and no lights. Sometimes, they slept in their car. César's family had once owned a big farm. Now they were migrants, working on other people's farms. César missed his life in Arizona. He wanted to go home.

One day, the Chávez family stopped at a restaurant to get something to eat. The owner told them to go away. He did not want Mexicans in his restaurant. It was the first time someone refused to serve César because of his skin color. This is called discrimination. César knew it was not right.

He soon saw more discrimination. Stores had signs in the window that said WHITES ONLY. It meant that only white people could shop there. In movie theaters, Mexicans and blacks could not sit near whites. They had to sit in a separate area. César's school was only for Mexican and black children. There was a different school for the white children.

The Chávez family was very poor and did not have many clothes. César's sister Rita dropped out of

Everyone—even young children—had to work in the fields.

WHITES ONLY
MEXICANS AND NEGROES STAY OUT

César with some of his brothers, sisters, and friends on the family car.

school at age twelve because she felt ashamed that she had no shoes. César had to quit school at the end of eighth grade. His father had been in a car accident, and the family needed César's help. Now he had to work every day from morning to night, picking crops to earn money for food. His mother was sad. She wished César could stay in school. She did not know how to read or write, and she knew that an education was very important.

César at his eighth-grade graduation.

✳3✳

"Get Out
If You Can"

In 1946, César turned nineteen and joined the United States Navy. He was tired of farm work. Would his life be better in the navy? As a sailor on a ship in the Pacific Ocean, he saw discrimination again. Blacks and Latinos had to work as cooks or painters. They were not allowed to do other jobs.

One day when César had time off from the navy, he went

César in the U.S. Navy

to the movies. He sat in the whites-only section. The police arrested him because he would not move to the "colored" section. It was the first time César went to jail, but it was not the last. He would be arrested many times in his life for speaking out. He wanted justice for everyone.

When César's time in the navy was over, he went home to California. César married Helen Fabela in 1948. They moved to a poor neighborhood in San José called *Sal Si Puedes* ("Get Out If You Can"). Like César, Helen was a migrant worker who dreamed of a better life.

César and Helen

César wanted to help people with their problems. In 1952 he stopped working in the fields. He got a job with a group called the Community Service

Organization (CSO). Working for the CSO, César went door-to-door to talk to people about voting. Voting is very important because it gives people the power to pick the country's leaders.

César and Helen also taught people to read and write. Some of their neighbors were from Mexico. César encouraged them to take classes so they could pass the test to become American citizens. César

Working for the Community Service Organization (CSO), César told farmworkers to vote in elections.

Helen and César with six of their eight children.

learned many useful skills at the CSO. He became more confident in himself.

César never forgot what it was like to be a farmworker out in the fields all day. In 1962, he decided to follow his dream of helping farmworkers. By then, he and Helen had eight children. The eldest was thirteen. He left the Community Service Organization and moved from San José to Delano, California.

For years, he had helped people living in cities. Now it was time to help the migrants.

4

¡Huelga! Strike!

César believed that people had more power working in groups than they did working alone. He said that a union could help the migrants. A union is a group of workers who come together to solve problems. Migrants had many problems. In the fields, they had no clean water to drink. They needed time to rest and go to the bathroom. Their workday was too long, and their pay was too low.

In 1962, César started a union called the National Farm Workers Association (NFWA). Later, it would be called the United Farm Workers (UFW). At first, César's union had only a few members. He traveled all over the state, talking to farmworkers. As more people joined the union, it grew and grew.

César learned about important leaders like Mahatma Gandhi in India and Martin Luther King, Jr. They did not believe in violence. Instead they used peaceful ways to work for change. César liked their ideas. He wanted to try some of them in the fight for migrant workers' rights.

On September 8, 1965, Filipino grape pickers went on strike. This means they walked out of the vineyards where they were picking grapes. They said they would not go back to work until they had fair pay. The

When grape pickers went on strike, they asked everyone not to buy grapes.

members of César's union decided they would join the Filipino workers and go on strike too.

The police arrested many people during the strike. It was not against the law to go on strike, but the police said they were making too much noise. Some people were arrested just for shouting *"¡Huelga!"* (*Huelga* is Spanish for "strike.") César used a loudspeaker to ask migrants in the fields to stop working and join the strike. The police said he was talking too loud, so they took him to jail.

César called the flag of the NFWA "a strong, beautiful sign of hope."

In the vineyards, grapes rotted on the vine. The vineyard owners were mad because they were losing a lot of money. But they would not talk with the union.

On March 17, 1966, César and seventy strikers began to walk to Sacramento, the capital of California. They wanted everyone to know about the farmworkers' long hours, hard work, and low wages. The strikers carried the flag of the NFWA. It was red

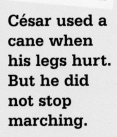

By marching, the strikers could get more attention.

César used a cane when his legs hurt. But he did not stop marching.

with a black eagle in a white circle. Under that flag, they walked about three hundred miles. Along the way, many people joined them. When the march reached Sacramento on April 11, 1966, the group had ten thousand people. Still, the vineyard owners would not give in.

Next, César called for Americans all across the country to stop buying California grapes. This is called a boycott. If growers could not sell their grapes, they would lose even more money. Would the growers ever listen?

César would not use violence. He believed that words could be stronger than fists.

César's dogs Huelga and Boycott took good care of him. He said they brought him good luck.

✺5✺

Champion of the People

César had one more plan to draw attention to the migrants' problems: He stopped eating. This is called a fast, or a hunger strike. César was showing everyone that he was ready to risk his life to help the farmworkers. He did not eat for twenty-five days. Many people heard about César's hunger strike. They joined the boycott and stopped buying grapes. Important leaders such as Martin Luther King, Jr., told César that they agreed with his fight for justice.

Because of the strike, the march, the boycott, and César's fast, the owners of the grape farms in

César would not give up.

César

California finally said yes to César's union. In 1970 the owners agreed to treat their workers better and pay them more. It was a great victory for César and for the farmworkers in California.

By 1972 César's union had sixty thousand members. The union kept on fighting to make life better for migrants. Over the years, César led more nonviolent protests.

At last! After the strike, César signed the deal for better pay for farmworkers.

In 1975 California passed a law against the short-handled hoe. This terrible tool would no longer be used in the fields. For César, this was another big victory. It had taken seven years to win the battle against the short-handled hoe. He was very happy.

Migrants called the hoe "El Cortito," the Short One.

In the 1980s, César began to worry about pesticides. Pesticides are poisons that are sprayed on farmers' fields to kill insects that eat the crops. Were the pesticides making the farmworkers sick? Could eating grapes sprayed with pesticides make people sick? César went into action. His

César said pesticides were bad for people.

Once again, César asked everyone to stop buying grapes.

union made a movie to teach people about the dangers of pesticides. Once again, César asked people everywhere to boycott grapes. Then he started another fast. He did not eat anything for thirty-six days.

César was right about pesticides. But it would be many years before the government made laws to protect people and workers from these poisons.

All his life, César worked to help others. For this, he received many honors and many awards. Buildings, streets, and libraries all over the United States are named in his honor.

In 1993, César Chávez died in San Luis, Arizona. He was sixty-six years old. He had eight children and 27 grandchildren. A year after César died, President

Bill Clinton gave him the U.S. Medal of Freedom. It is the highest award for a citizen of the United States. His wife, Helen, thanked the president. The same year, California honored César in a special way. His birthday became a state holiday. Now, every year on March 31, people in California celebrate the birth of a man who fought for farmworkers and was a hero of working people everywhere.

A César Chávez stamp came out in 2003.

César did not believe in violence, yet he fought hard all his life. César changed the way Mexican Americans were treated. He improved the lives of migrant farmworkers. There is still more work to be done, but César Chávez planted the seeds of change.

More than anything else, César cared about helping others. "All my life, I have been driven by one dream," he said.

❊ Timeline ❊

1927 Born on March 31 near Yuma, Arizona.

1938 Chávez family loses its farm and goes to California to find work.

1946 César joins the navy.

1948 Marries Helen Fabela on October 22.

1952 Works for the Community Service Organization.

1962 Starts the National Farm Workers Association, a union to help migrant farmworkers.

1965 César's union goes on strike.

1966 César and union members go on a protest march.

1967 Asks people all over the country to boycott grapes.

1986 Protests the use of pesticides on crops.

1993 Dies on April 23 in San Luis, Arizona.

☀ Words to Know ☀

boycott—To stop buying something as a means of protest.

discrimination—Treating someone unfairly because of race, age, sex, or religion.

fast—To go without food to bring attention to a problem. Also called a *hunger strike*.

Filipino—A person from the Philippine Islands in Southeast Asia.

migrant worker—A person who goes from one area to another to find work, especially picking farm crops.

protest march—To call attention to a problem by marching in the streets.

strike—To stop working, usually to demand higher pay or better working conditions.

union—A group of workers who join together to make deals with their bosses.

vineyards—Fields where grapes grow.

Learn More

Books

Bernier-Grand, Carmen T. *César: Sí, Se Puede! = Yes, We Can!* New York: Marshall Cavendish, 2004.

Krull, Kathleen. *Harvesting Hope: The Story of César Chávez.* San Diego: Harcourt, Inc., 2003.

Soto, Gary. *César Chávez: A Hero for Everyone.* New York: Simon & Schuster, 2003.

Internet Addresses

The César E. Chávez Foundation
<http://www.cesarchavezfoundation.org>
At the left, click on "César Chávez" for a biography and photos.

United Farmworkers of America
<http://www.ufw.org/history.htm>
Click on "The Story of César Chávez" or "César Chávez Chronology" for lots of information. (This Web site is in Spanish, too.)

The Library of Congress presents "America's Story"
<www.americaslibrary.gov>
Click on the Search star halfway down the page. Then type in "César Chávez" to learn more about this American hero.

✳ Index ✳